Table of Contents

Introduction

Most people will tell you that they want to improve themselves and grow emotionally. This process of introspection and self-reflection is never easy. It requires the ability to understand and handle your emotions in a healthy manner, and this always takes time and patience. That is why this book, *"Emotional Intelligence: Exploring the Most Powerful Intelligence Ever Discovered,"* has been written just for you. This book is meant to help make the process of emotional development clearer and smoother.

Our lives are filled with constant and continual situations where communication with others is necessary. Your ability to communicate effectively and successfully with others is what sets you apart from animals. However, how many of us actually take the time to think about just how important the way we communicate is? In what ways can we become better able to communicate? This would be a good time to introduce you to the concept of emotional intelligence.

Emotional intelligence, or EI, is defined as the ability to recognize, control, and express your emotions in a way that enables you to handle interpersonal relationships empathetically and judiciously. Emotional intelligence is what enables you to recognize how others are feeling in a given situation, differentiate the myriad of emotions, and act accordingly. It is only through emotional intelligence that we are able to adjust our emotions as we go through life, thus reaching whatever goals we have set.

Nobody can claim that they do not have emotional intelligence. The only difference is that people exhibit varying levels of EI – some are simply more emotionally intelligent than others. However, it is not something that is fixed from birth to death. There are steps and actions you can take to become more intelligent emotionally. In fact, if there is one feature of personal development that most people need to work on, it is their emotional intelligence.

Research has proven that those individuals who have a higher emotional quotient, or EQ, tend to make better leaders, enjoy a better quality of personal and professional relationships, and are more mentally healthy. All you need to do to increase your emotional quotient is take the time to put into practice the tips and strategies outlined in this book.

In here, you will learn how to know yourself better so that you can understand others better. You will learn how your emotional brain works, and how emotional intelligence can be improved. There are some great tools and tips described in this book, so make sure that you are ready to learn and practice them. Get ready to also learn about some of the new discoveries in the field of emotional intelligence.

EMOTIONAL INTELLIGENCE

Exploring the Most Powerful Intelligence Ever Discovered

I hope that this book provides you with everything you need, and then some. Let's go ahead and get emotionally smarter!

If you are someone who is on the journey of personal development or self improvement I would highly recommend you read the book MINDSET: How Positive Thinking Will Set You Free & Help You Achieve Massive Success In Life, by Benjamin Smith.

Also don't forget to claim your FREE bonus at the end of this book!

Chapter 1: You and Your Emotional Brain

Before we can even begin to learn or understand the concept of emotional intelligence, we must first explore the two components that make up the word – *emotions* and *intelligence*.

Over the last three centuries, psychologists have been able to define three distinct parts of the human mind: thoughts, emotions, and motivations. Thoughts, also known as cognition, include regular functions such as memory, judgment, and reasoning. This is where intelligence comes in because it is used to measure your cognitive functions. Emotions, on the other hand, include things like moods, feelings, and evaluations. Motivations refer to behaviors that you learn or biological urges. They are not relevant in the scope of this book so we shall not go into them for now.

In order to explore the links between your emotions and your thoughts, it is important to fully understand emotions and how they affect your life.

What are Emotions?

Emotions are simply mental reactions characterized by strong feeling and corresponding physical effects. They can also be described as powerful social signals that send us messages to spur us to respond to our environment. Emotions help us communicate either in a voluntary or non-voluntary manner, thus facilitating our social interactions.

Significance of Emotions

So what is the significance or purpose of having emotions? As human beings, we have developed a specific number of emotional reactions that are triggered by conditions or situations. If you are facing a particular problem, your emotions can help you galvanize your thoughts and figure out a solution. So one of the most significant purposes of emotions is to identify dependable cues, then activate reactions that you may have relied on in the past to solve similar problems.

Let's take the example of fear as an emotion. If you are walking the streets at night and fear that you might get mugged at a particular spot, your emotion will trigger a specific routine. First of all, your sight and hearing will instantly become more attentive. Then all your other body systems, for example, hunger and thirst, will be suppressed in exchange for physical safety. Your brain will start focusing on specific bits of information gathered from your environment.

You start to analyze options in form of safe versus dangerous rather than easy versus hard. You start remembering previous situations you have faced similar to the one you are in now. If you see someone step out of a dark alley and start running toward you, fear may either force you to shout for help or paralyze you completely. You then try to determine current as well as future actions that both you and the assailant might take. Finally, your physiological system will kick in and you either fight or flee.

From the example above, you can quickly see that emotions help to mobilize entire systems to influence your goals, priorities, focus, perceptions, and physiology.

Emotions also inform you of how the people around you are experiencing a certain situation. They tell you the perspective that you and others have concerning the meaning of things. Most emotions are attached to some kind of automatic signal, but some are more complex and do not exhibit any unique signals, for example, envy or guilt.

Recognizing Emotions

Scientists have generally concluded that there are six basic and distinct emotions. These are fear, disgust, anger, surprise, sadness, and happiness. When it comes to non-verbal emotions, it is somewhat possible to recognize unique facial expressions linked to any one of the basic emotions. It is important to note that these emotions are not taught or learned – they just manifest the same way in people regardless of the culture they grew up in. Even blind people, display the same facial emotions as people with sight!

So is it possible to control your emotions and how you express them, and if so, to what extent? The truth is that some emotions and expressions are more easily controlled than others. For example, you may find it easy to control your body movements and gestures, but it is very difficult to maintain a high level of control over your pulse rate or dilated pupils. Research has even shown that we tend to leak emotions when stressed, through leg movements and gestures.

The tone of voice also gives away a person's emotional state. This allows you to decode sounds that others make. Body posture, eye gaze patterns, and spatial behavior are also clues into a person's emotional state. In general, it is believed that non-verbal cues provide the best way to judge a person's emotions since they are more difficult to fake.

Emotional Intelligence

Emotional intelligence is one of the major aspects that determine how you relate to the people around you. Everyone is emotionally intelligent in his or her own way, but some people seem to have a higher level than others. The level of your emotional intelligence can be represented by a score on a standardized test and is referred to as *Emotional Quotient* (EQ). Your EQ can be improved if you use some methods that have been designed to improve emotional intelligence.

One of the most holistic ways to define emotional intelligence is: "The capacity to perceive, access, and generate emotions in order to think clearer, understand emotional knowledge, and regulate emotions in a way that enhances intellectual and emotional growth." This definition takes into account the concept that your emotions should lead to intelligent thinking, and you should also think intelligently about your emotions. It is clear that there is no separating intelligence and emotion.

Emotional intelligence enables you to make better decisions based on what you are feeling under a given situation. It also helps to connect to others in ways that show that you care about them and the way they feel. Having a high EQ enables you to identify and control your emotions in a positive way, thus enhancing effective communication. A person with a greater EQ is able to cope with the daily stresses and struggles of life, and neutralize any potential conflicts, even as they continually empathize with others around them.

Emotional Quotient (EQ) versus Intelligence Quotient (IQ)

There is a huge difference between EQ and IQ:

- Your IQ is inborn, which means we all start out at different and unique levels of intelligence. Some kids learn to play the piano or read a book really early in life, while others take longer to master such skills. Your IQ, or cognitive intelligence, is your ability to think rationally, act purposefully, and handle your environment effectively. It is measured through an IQ test, which tests your rational, analytical, logical, and intellectual abilities. It also focuses on your skills in mathematical, verbal, visual, and spatial tasks. A person with a high IQ – the average IQ is 100 – is usually able to understand new concepts quickly, retain and recall information, reason well, think abstractly, and solve problems.

- EQ, on the other hand, is something that you learn over time. We all start out as babies with the same emotional intelligence, but depending on our environment, we gradually improve our EQ throughout life. It is measured using various tests and assessments, such as EQ-i, EQ-360, and MSCEIT. These tests are discussed in more detail in chapter 3.

Emotional intelligence has nothing to do with intellectual ability. No matter how high or low your intelligence is, or how old you are, you can still improve your emotional quotient. The only thing you must commit to is applying it in your everyday life, which may be difficult for some more than others. It is not easy changing one's behavior for good. You must be willing to put in the hard work of learning how to handle stress and staying emotionally aware. However, it is definitely worth it.

Why Emotional Intelligence is Important

Intellectual aptitude is not the major factor in achieving a balanced and fulfilled life. There are a lot of smart people out there who are totally clueless when it comes to maintaining both professional and personal relationships. A high IQ may get people's attention and you through the door, but it is your EQ that will determine how successful you are with regard to handling stress and others emotions ever day.

The best strategy to adopt is to find a way to get your IQ and EQ working harmoniously together. This will require you to commit to continuous self-improvement and introspection so that you can gradually create a better life. Being able to assess, control, and manage your emotions under a given situation is very critical to living a successful and happy life.

There is always room for improvement when it comes to emotional intelligence. Improving your EQ is not just for maladjusted nerds and people with social or personality issues. Everyone can gain something from this. You could be a person who is quite socially aware with good social skills, but you have problems managing your relationships. Alternatively, you could be great at dealing with your personal emotions and relationships but lack the necessary social awareness and skills. It is always best to first understand where you are weak before working on improving yourself.

Chapter 2: How Emotional Intelligence Works

Now that we understand what emotional intelligence is and its significance in your life, let's examine how it works. In this chapter, we are going to look at the intricacies and inner workings that define your emotional intelligence. It is important to begin by first learning how emotional intelligence links to your self-perception.

Knowing Thyself

Since emotional intelligence involves your personal emotions, and your emotions form a key part of who you are, you must then learn to understand yourself. If you see yourself in a positive and healthy way, you will definitely find it easier to confidently establish stronger relationships, manage stress, and achieve your goals. The way you see and know yourself is also referred to as *self-perception*.

The majority of people think they know themselves but in reality, most don't spend enough time understanding who they really are. Most people usually go through an emotional outburst without later reflecting on the causes and effects of those emotions. Self-perception is important because it allows you to figure out who you are. It also enables you to determine how to close the gap between your present personality and who you want to be.

A person who is not aware of who they are can never be able to know or understand those around them. If you plan on improving your emotional intelligence, you must learn to enhance your self-awareness.

This process begins by writing down in a journal what you feel every day. Note down your emotions at specific intervals throughout the day, making sure to write the causes of your emotions. At the end of the day, go over what you have written. This is a very effective way to determine the patterns your emotions have developed. You will, therefore, be able to take a closer and keener look into your life, the emotions you go through, and the people or events that trigger those emotions. This is the best way to learn how to manage your emotions and find ways of using them to your benefit.

The concept of self-perception can be analyzed from three distinct viewpoints:

1. Self-regard

This refers to taking care of your own needs first without coming across as being insecure or egotistical. Learn what your strengths are and use them to your advantage. This is important because a person who has a high self-regard will find it easier to respect others. If you are unsure of how to gauge your self-regard, get a group of people you trust and who know you very well to give you feedback. Once you have the right and honest information, then you can start taking action based on what you now know about yourself.

2. Self-awareness

This refers to knowing your own emotions and how they impact on the people around you. Self-awareness also helps to identify the non-verbal emotional cues from other people. If you are highly self-aware, you will realize that you are able to maintain more meaningful relationships than someone who is not.

The best way to practice and improve self-awareness is by reading the facial expressions of other people around you. You can also closely monitor their body language during times of emotional outbursts. To make this exercise as effective as possible, make sure that you are not actively participating in the emotional situation. Once the emotional exchange has ended, run the scene over in your mind, analyzing how you would have handled the situation had you been actively involved. This exercise provides a great way to prepare for the times when you will be engaged in an emotional confrontation yourself.

3. Self-actualization

This refers to striving to achieve your life's purpose, whether it is professional or personal in nature. You need to find the things that give meaning to your life and go after them. This requires a certain degree of courage that most people can rarely muster. You have to make bold decisions and take committed action in order to attain self-actualization.

What you need to do is take a long hard look at your talents, strengths, and skills. Learn what they are and then put them to work to achieve your dreams. Discover ways of leveraging your passions for your own good as well as the people around you.

Mindfulness is one of the most popular ways of training your mind to improve your self-perception. Mindfulness simply refers to being aware of the things happening around you at any given time. For example, if you are enjoying a meal, you can practice mindful eating, where you chew slowly as you savor the taste of every ingredient in the food. This way, you get to constantly interact more intimately with your emotional state.

You will learn how to be able to take a step back from an emotional exchange and determine what your true emotions are, before reacting. Mindfulness is effective in self-perception because your mind is taught how to focus on what matters the most at that particular time, paying full attention to yourself and the things around you.

Understanding the Roots of Empathy

Empathy can be considered to be one of the cornerstones of emotional intelligence. You cannot claim to be emotionally intelligent and yet you have no empathy. Empathy is what creates the connection between you and other people, whether it's your partner, kids, friends, or anyone who is close to you. It can even help you manage conflicts with people who are intentionally difficult to work with.

Most people assume that empathy is fixed, but the truth is that anyone can be taught how to be more empathetic. All you need is a bit of practice.

What is empathy, really?

Most people get confused when asked to differentiate between empathy and sympathy. They are not the same thing. Sympathy is where you tell someone that you care about what they are going through. For example, if Jack's mother passes away, you approach him and say, "Jack, I'm very sorry about your mother's death." This is a noble and considerate gesture that demonstrates that you care about what happened to Jack. However, notice that the statement starts with "I" – you have made it about you!

This is where the difference between sympathy and empathy comes in. Empathy is where you put the emotions of the other person first. For example, "Jack, you must be devastated by the loss of your mother." Notice how you started by acknowledging how Jack feels at the moment? Empathy is never about your own feelings, but understanding the emotions that another faces.

Why is it so important to understand the difference between these two emotions? Sympathy is used whenever you want to show someone how you feel about a tragic situation they are going through. It shows that you care and want them to feel comforted. In other words, sympathy is clearly an end in itself.

Empathy, however, is quite the opposite in the sense that it is an opener. You show empathy when you want to get to know another person better and gain their trust. It is more than just expressing caring for their current situation, but wanting to deeply understand what they are going through. Empathy enhances relationships and helps you become more personally involved with someone. You strive to know the person and strengthen the bond with them. Unlike sympathy, empathy is the beginning of an interaction.

Most people in today's society are very good at expressing sympathy when tragedy strikes and this is evident in the use of social media. People jump at the chance to send messages of condolence to people affected by tsunamis, hurricanes, earthquakes, famine, and floods all over the world. However, what is severely lacking is genuine empathy that goes beyond mere "I" statements to "You" statements. How many people do you know who are truly and naturally empathetic? Practice and develop your empathy skills and you will definitely stand out from the crowd.

Understanding the Four Skills of Emotional Intelligence

There are generally four key skills that you need to develop in order to give you the ability to handle whatever situation in an emotionally intelligent way.

1. Self-awareness
This is where you learn how to identify your own emotions and recognize the impact that they have on both your thoughts and actions. The more you know yourself and understand your emotional states, the greater your ability to display confidence in yourself. This will put you in a good position to enhance your emotional intelligence.

2. Self-management
This is your ability to control the spontaneous feelings, behaviors, and urges that come upon you at any given moment. The main goal of self management is to be able to handle your emotions, whenever they crop up, in a healthy and productive manner. You should also develop the ability to adapt to new and unanticipated circumstances and ensure that all commitments are followed through.

3. Social awareness
You need to be able to understand what other people around you are feeling, as well as their concerns and needs. Social awareness is linked to being comfortable in social settings where you interact with others, read their emotional cues, and realize the kind of traits they have.

4. Relationship management
This is where you develop the ability to maintain healthy and strong relationships. You have to learn how to inspire and influence people, be an effective communicator, manage or resolve conflicts, and become a team player.

How Emotional Intelligence Can Impact Your Life

You now know the skills that emotional intelligence requires. However, it is also important to understand the areas in your life that will benefit from being more emotionally intelligent. These are:

1. **Mental health** – Your emotional intelligence plays a major part in how you perceive the world around you and the actions you take. If you develop a high emotional intelligence, then you will experience a greater sense of mental wellness, manifesting itself through less stress and more confidence.

2. **Physical wellbeing** – You may have noticed that every time your emotions become unbalanced or uncontrolled, your physical health deteriorates. Emotional intelligence is able to put you in a position where you handle your emotions in a healthy manner, thus improving your physical wellbeing.

3. **Relationships** – This is an important area of our lives and we must learn how to understand the feelings of others. Once you have developed the ability to tune into your own emotions, you will find it easier to convey those feelings to the people around you. Emotional intelligence helps you recognize what people are feeling, thus enabling you to treat them well just as you would want to be treated.

4. **Prosperity** – This is not only about financial success. Prosperity encompasses setting goals, going after them, and achieving them. Developing a high level of emotional intelligence is one of the best ways to fast-track your journey to prosperity. You will be bolder and more confident when chasing your dreams. Time wasting and procrastination will be a thing of the past, as you will have the focus and strength to see your commitments through. In order to achieve success in the future, you will obviously have to make great sacrifices today, and a high EQ helps you understand this clearly.

Are You Emotionally Unintelligent?

One of the most significant ways to identify a person who is emotionally unintelligent is their low self-awareness. Such a person may be around a group of other people but they will have no idea how out of sync they are with everyone else. The sad reality of being low in emotional intelligence is that you won't realize how others perceive you. What's worse, you may not be aware of why your life and relationships are so difficult.

Emotionally unintelligent people exhibit behaviors that make them their own worst enemy. Due to their low empathy, inability to control their impulses, and poor social skills, everything they do tends to be self-defeating. They are rarely happy, can't resolve their own problems, and find it very hard to set and achieve their life goals.

It is important to note that these attributes bring about real-life complications. People with low EQ tend to have problems maintaining any kind of meaningful or intimate relationships, can't hold jobs for long, are rarely promoted at their workplace, and find it difficult to handle stress. Another key thing to note is that being smart intellectually doesn't mean you cannot have low EQ. Some people have extremely high IQ but very low EQ.

It is not easy recognizing someone who has low emotional intelligence because most people have become very good at faking EI skills. Some people are able to cover up their inadequacies through superficial means. Just because a person says that they are aware of themselves and those around them doesn't make it true.

Here are some of the general signs of emotionally unintelligent people:

- Easily get angry without realizing it and why they feel so

- Are not aware of the impact of their behavior on others

- Cannot understand the feelings of others

- Are often self-centered

- Find it difficult to control any emotion, more so when stressed

- Make other people behave just as badly as they do

- Find it difficult to maintain existing relationships or meet new people

- Overestimate their abilities and skills

- Are avoided by most people

Is someone who is emotionally unintelligent a hopeless case? No, they are not. Everyone can learn how to raise his or her EQ given the right training. If you have just discovered that you fit the description outlined above, do not worry. That is why you have this book. The chapters that follow cover how to measure your current EQ and what you can practically do to improve your overall emotional intelligence.

Chapter 3: Assessing and Improving Emotional Intelligence

In this chapter, you will learn some of the most popular assessment tests that are used to measure emotional intelligence, as well as some of the techniques that have proved useful when developing your EQ.

Measuring Emotional Intelligence

There are three general test categories that psychologists use to measure a person's emotional intelligence. These tests have been validated and standardized by psychologists and researchers. They are:

Self-report tests

These tests require you to answer a few questions and then your response is compared to others on an online database. The questions generally cover topics dealing with your self-perception, your social interactions, and your mood swings. One of the most popularly used self-report tests is the EQ-i.

The EQ-i (Emotional Quotient Inventory) was the first published emotional intelligence test to be used all over the world. It is now available in more than 30 different languages, with thousands of people all over the world already having taken the test. You will be able to compare your results with people in your local geographical area and culture. This test is considered very valid and reliable.

The EQ-i test covers five key areas of your emotional and social life. These are:

- Intra-personal areas – The test examines your capacity to understand and manage yourself. It focuses on your self-awareness, assertiveness, independence, self-regard, and self-actualization.

- Inter-personal areas – This focuses on your ability to interact with others and get along with them. Interpersonal areas include your interpersonal relationships, social responsibility, and empathy.

- Adaptability – In this area, the test examines your ability to adapt, be flexible, and solve everyday problems as they come up. The factors affecting adaptability include reality testing, flexibility, and problem solving.

- Stress management – In this area, the test examines your capacity to absorb stress and manage your impulses. The factors measured include stress tolerance and impulse control.

- General mood – In this area, the test focuses on your ability to stay positive regardless of your circumstances. The factors analyzed include optimism and happiness.

360-degree assessments
This is an assessment that takes into account the views of your close family, friends, work colleagues, bosses, and etc. They are all asked to report and rate you depending on how they perceive your behavior in the same areas that you rated yourself. For example, you may perceive yourself to be very social and interactive, but some of the people around you may have a differing perspective. The most popular 360-degree assessment test is known as EQ-360.

The EQ-360 is used by psychologists to measure a person's emotional intelligence by way of collecting the input of others who know the subject very well. It is used in conjunction with the EQ-i test. The EQ-360 involves comparing the subjects' own ratings with the ratings of others. A qualified professional should conduct this test.

This test gives a well-rounded perspective of your emotional intelligence. Some of the factors that are measured include:

- Kindness
- Sensitivity
- Expressiveness
- Optimism
- Self-control
- Independence
- Caring nature
- Stress-management

Performance tests
These work like your regular IQ test as they measure your emotional quotient as if it were an ability. You may be shown photos of people and asked to determine the corresponding emotions. You may also be presented with a complex real-life challenge and asked to respond. Your response is then compared to those of others who have taken the test. One of the most common performance tests used is MSCEIT.

MSCEIT stands for the Mayer, Salovey, and Caruso Emotional Intelligence Test. It is named after the two psychology professors who sparked research into emotions as a form of intelligence. There is no test that is more widely used to gauge emotional intelligence than the MSCEIT. Unlike the two previous tests described above, the MSCEIT examines a totally different set of areas and factors. There are generally four broad branches that this test focuses on:

1. Perceiving emotion

This is one of the most basic areas of EI and involves receiving and expressing emotions non-verbally. It is believed that emotional expression was a key component of early man's ability to communicate with others in social settings. Back then, and to this day, it is possible to perceive emotions of anger, sadness, or fear from the look on a person's face. Researchers, scientists, and biologists have all made great strides in understanding how people recognize and display emotions. Your ability to accurately discern how others are feeling, whether it is through their voice or face, is the first step in understanding more complex emotions.

2. Using emotions to guide thinking

Your emotions have the capacity to guide how you think and promote thought. For example, whatever you find yourself reacting to emotionally must be something that grabbed your attention. This means that whatever you are feeling right now as you read this book will direct your thinking. You could be enjoying what you are currently learning about EI and consequently focus on positive thoughts. If you feel bored or let down by the content, your thinking will turn negative. It is also important to note that that being emotional can be very beneficial for some creative endeavors. A good example is painters, authors, musicians, and artists, who do their best work when either extremely positive or negative.

3. Understanding emotions

It is not enough to just perceive emotions in yourself or others. It is equally crucial that you be able to comprehend these emotions and potential reactions. We all know that emotions relay information, with every emotion having its own unique pattern of messages and potential actions. For example, if you are angry, the message is that you believe that you have not been treated fairly. Your potential reactions could include instantly attacking the person you feel has offended you, peacefully informing them of how you feel, seeking revenge at a later time, or withdrawing from the situation to calm yourself down.

The moment you are able to identify the emotion, its message, and potential actions, you will have a greater ability to logically reason and communicate effectively.

Understanding emotions must always involve comprehending the message behind the emotion and reasoning out the meaning.

4. Managing emotions

This is the final branch of EI. You need to know that your emotions are manageable, but this will only be possible once the above three branches have been grasped. The ideal situation is where you are able to experience emotional signals without being overwhelmed by those that are too painful to bear. It is important to find a place of balance where you have an emotional comfort zone. This zone will help you control and manage your own and others' emotions in order to achieve both personal and social objectives. The exact tools and strategies used to manage emotions are discussed in a later chapter.

These three tests give a clear representation of your real-life behavior under given circumstances. They can be used to predict how you will handle stressful situations, as well as your strengths and weaknesses. When these test results are combined, you will be able to get an accurate picture of yourself, how others perceive you, and your competence on tasks relating to emotional intelligence. Once you take these tests and analyze your results, you will have taken the first step in enhancing your emotional intelligence. As long as an EQ test is done using reliable testing techniques, you will obtain extremely useful information about your emotional intelligence.

Understanding EQ Tests

EQ tests have been developed in a way that uses the same best practices that IQ tests have adopted. In an EQ test, you may be provided with a real-life situation that you may come across on any given day. You are then presented with a number of responses and told to pick the one that best suits you.

The major difference between an EQ and an IQ test is that the questions in an EQ test do not have a correct or incorrect answer. For example, in an IQ test, every question has a single correct answer. However, an EQ test presents possible answers that can be argued out by the respondent. In fact, you may be able to argue that all the responses presented are somewhat correct. The authors of an EQ test usually use two methods to decide how correct an answer is:

- **Norm groups** – This is where a group of more than 1000 people is surveyed as a sample population of those who will do the test in the future. The answer that garners the majority response is deemed to be the correct answer. This is a form of social consensus of what the right behavior should be.

- **Expert review** - This involves gathering a panel of renowned experts within the EI field. These should be men and women who have an understanding of basic and sophisticated EI theories. They must have performed research on emotions and provided some kind of contribution to the scientific literature of emotions. The correct response will be the one that the majority of experts agree on as being the best choice.

Chapter 4: Increasing Your Emotional Intelligence

In this chapter, you will learn the strategies that you can use to increase your emotional intelligence. This means that we will look into ways of recognizing negative emotions and managing your own various emotional states.

How to Recognize Negative Emotions

Negative emotions are simply those feelings that overwhelm you and prevent you from achieving whatever goals you have. They tend to interfere with your thoughts and actions. Since emotions are signals that send a message to your brain, you should view negative emotions that there is something wrong that you need to pay attention to.

The problem comes in when the negative feeling is so strong that it prevents you from taking any useful action. This is why most people usually wallow in the emotion itself rather than do something about the cause.

So how can you determine the cause of your negative emotions? One way is through the ABCDE theory. This theory is also known as Rational Emotive Behavior Theory and was developed in the 1950s by a psychologist called Dr. Albert Ellis. The ABCDE theory splits emotional upset or disturbance into five parts:

- **Activating event (A)** – This is an external event that people use as an excuse for their problems. For example, being insulted by someone, losing your job, or being dumped by your girlfriend.

- **Beliefs (B)** – It is common to find a person blaming the activating event for their anger, sadness, or frustration. However, this is a false viewpoint because what actually causes the negative emotions are the beliefs that they have chosen to adopt. It is what you tell yourself about the activating event that is the problem. If you got fired from your job, you may believe that it's because you are a poor employee. It is the belief that is the cause of your negative emotion, not the fact that you have been let go.

- **Consequence (C)** – This usually comes in form of self-defeating emotions, such as anxiety or depression. When people talk about how they feel about a given situation, they tend to start by stating the consequence and then immediately jumping to the activating event as the cause. For example, someone might say that they feel depressed because they lost their job or got dumped. This is how the majority of people view their problems. They rarely figure out that it is the false belief that they have adopted that is making them feel the way they do.

- **Dispute (D)** – This is where you start to dispute your beliefs regarding the activating event. You begin to question every logical and illogical belief and thought about the event you went through.

- **Effect (E)** – Once you have calmed down your emotions, you will be able to relax your mind and body. This will allow you to mull over ideas on how to rationally resolve your current situation.

How to Manage your Own Emotions

Every day brings its own troubles. You know those days when everything just goes off script and makes you feel like staying under the covers for the rest of the day. Unfortunately, life does not allow us the luxury of burying our heads in the sand and ignoring the world around us. So what can you do to cope with your negative emotions and how can you make the best out of a bad situation? There are a number of effective tools that you can use to refocus your energies and manage your emotions better, such as:

Cognitive restructuring

This is a cognitive-behavioral approach that psychologists use to help patients manage their negative feelings. This form of therapy is based on the concept that "you are what you think." It is premised on the idea that you have to find a way to refute any cognitive distortions you may have.

Cognitive distortions are simply those thoughts that you repeat to yourself whenever something negative happens to you. They could be related to a person or a situation. Cognitive restructuring can help you resolve negative feelings such as low self-esteem, impulsiveness, social anxiety, and stress.

The steps below are used in the cognitive restructuring process:

1. Try to remember a time or situation where you went through negative emotions. Think about how you felt, your thoughts at the time, and how you behaved.

2. In your notebook, jot down these column headings:

    - Activating Event

- Feelings About Event
- Initial Thoughts
- Supporting Thoughts
- Non-supporting Thoughts
- Balanced Thoughts
- Mood
- Action Plan

3. Under Activating Event column, note the event or situation that caused your negative emotion.

4. Under the Feelings About Event column, write down how you felt about what happened. Record your emotions rather than your thoughts, preferably in a single word.

5. Under Initial Thoughts column, record what you initially thought regarding the situation.

6. Under the Supporting Thoughts column, note down anything that supports the thoughts you had initially. Then go to the Non-Supporting Thoughts column and write down any evidence that doesn't support your initial thoughts.

7. Under Balanced Thoughts, note down your conclusions once you have analyzed the situation. These should be the thoughts that you end up with once you have examined and carefully considered both the supporting and non-supporting thoughts. You can talk to someone else during this step so that you are better able to come up with fair and unbiased conclusions.

8. Under the Mood column, write down changes in feelings regarding the situation. If there is anything you can do about the situation, begin planning how to do that. If it's something that you cannot change, then change how you feel about it.

9. The Action Plan column is where you will record the follow-up actions you will take to make the situation move ahead. You also need to assign due dates for every task under your action plan.

The cognitive restructuring approach enables you to see and think about things differently, thus altering how you feel about a situation.

Using distraction techniques

There are times when your negative emotions threaten to overwhelm you and escape seems like the best way out. This should not be misconstrued as running away from responsibilities, but simply a way of stepping back from a stressful situation to think things over.

Here are some distractive techniques that can help you cope with situations that trigger negative feelings:

- Taking a walk
- Exercise
- Yoga
- Talking to a close companion
- Counting to ten slowly
- Listening to soothing music or sounds

Alternative techniques for improving your EQ

There are certain alternative techniques that can help you improve your mental and emotional condition. The best way to maximize the benefits of these techniques is to make them part of your daily lifestyle. This way you will be prepared to handle any emotional situation when it arises.

1. Acupressure

This is similar to acupuncture and Shiatsu massage. Use the steps blow to practice acupressure:

- Use your forefinger and thumb of one hand to squeeze the fleshy part between the forefinger and thumb of the other hand. Apply pressure for five seconds.

- Do the same for the other hand.

- Repeat the cycle a total of three times. The tens emotions you felt should recede.

2. Meditation

One of the most fundamental things that you must learn to do is controlling your emotional state. This may not be as easy as you think because your body is used to responding in a particular way every time a specific emotion is triggered. What you need to do is counteract these natural reactions by training your body and mind to stop and assess the emotion and its cause.

Practicing meditation can be a very effective way to achieve this. Daily meditation will help you learn how to calm yourself down even under stressful situations. This will not happen overnight and you must keep practicing every day until you are finally able to stay calm and clear-headed under stressful circumstances.

You can use whatever form of meditation that suits you. There are a number of different styles out there, so just pick the one that works best for you and start practicing every day.

3. Mindfulness

This technique compliments the practice of meditation. Mindfulness refers to always maintaining your awareness of every moment and everything around you. This is something that you have to do every day if you want to learn how to improve your self-awareness. It will also help you take a deeper interest in the people around you, especially their facial expressions and body language. This will enable you to forge stronger relationships and enhance your concentration.

Use the steps below to practice mindfulness:

- Sit comfortably in a chair or lie down.

- Focus all your thoughts on the present moment and only on what is happening then. Do this for as long as you can.

- Pay attention to your senses of hearing, touch, smell, taste, and even your breathing.

- Practice belly breathing. Draw in air gently and then out of your belly.

- Ignore all other thoughts and focus only on deep and gentle breaths.

4. Affirmations

This is a great tool to use when you need some encouraging or inspiring words to empower you. Whenever you feel like your emotional state is getting out of control, grab your list of affirmations and read them out loud. Do this every day and it will put you in a more positive mindset.

To change your emotions for the better, you must practice the techniques described above. You should be in control of your emotions and not the other way around. Think of the techniques as a way of getting into emotional shape, the same way that you go to the gym or play a sport. Practice is what makes the difference between success and failure. Make a commitment to practice mindfulness, relaxation, meditation, cognitive restructuring, or any of the methods explained here. Do it every day and you will greatly improve your emotional intelligence.

Chapter 5: Developing Emotionally Intelligent Relationships

In this chapter, we will look into how to become more emotionally intelligent in your intimate relationships with family, spouses, and friends. These are special relationships that require conscious maintenance and nurturing. There are steps and tools that you can use to improve your close relationships.

Assessing your Romantic Relationships

Research shows that people who have a high EQ are more likely to enjoy satisfying and happier relationships. They are better able to manage their own and others emotions, leading to greater respect and trust.

When it comes to married couples, emotional intelligence matters a lot. Studies have revealed that there are specific areas that have the greatest impact on a marriage. They are:

- **Happiness** – This has been shown to have the highest correlation to marital satisfaction. You might think that a good marriage will breed happiness, but it is actually the other way around. It is only two happy people who can create a good marriage.

- **Self-regard** – People who regard themselves better are more adept at handling criticism than insecure people. Having such confidence prevents you from taking offense when negative comments are made.

- **Self-actualization** – People who are constantly seeking to make themselves better tend to be happier in their relationships.

- **Realism** – If you are realistic about the relationship you are in, you are less likely to be disappointed.

It is also important to rate your relationship so that both parties can see the areas that need to be worked on. You can write down how you rate your feelings on a scale of 1 to 5, and then record what you like the most about your relationship. You should also identify the areas of the relationship that you are not very happy about, and use a scale of 1 to 5 to rate just how much you want those changes to happen.

Using a rating helps you attach emotions to the different aspects of your relationship. Emotions are what hold a relationship together, so if you are determined to understand each other's emotions, then you will be able to build and strengthen your relationship.

The Role of Emotions in Relationship Growth

If you can control your emotions, you will be able to make your relationships stronger. Furthermore, managing the emotions of others also helps everyone focus on how to make the relationship better. Always try to maintain a sense of happiness so that you can be able to get over the rough bumps in the road. Avoid giving the people around you negativity because it breaks down the level of positive interaction between people.

Positive interaction between people is more than just verbal communication. Studies have shown that couples who focus more on communication than actual behavioral change were less happy in their relationships. Those who were in the habit of taking positive actions toward one another experienced happier and positive emotions in their relationships. In other words, doing good deeds for your partner will help improve the relationship and create more trust.

What makes couples grow apart emotionally is the fact that they start to take each other for granted. Life and busyness tend to get in the way and soon, you grow apart. Having a high level of emotional intelligence will help you maintain a good relationship because you have the skills to manage your own emotions and consequently those of your partner.

Managing your Partner's Feelings

It is extremely beneficial to learn how to manage your partner's emotions. It will help you learn how to read their emotions better and keep the relationship steady. The first step is usually to recognize their emotions. Can you tell when your partner is bored, suspicious, angry, or embarrassed? How do you measure their emotional temperature? Here's how:

- Pay attention to their tone of voice

- Watch their facial expressions

- Read their body language

- Ask them how they are feeling

- Use empathetic language to communicate

It is only when you are able to read your partner that you will stand a chance of managing their emotions. If they are in a negative mood, you need to know how to deal with their emotions. Here are some tips:

- If the conversation becomes too hot, agree to talk about the issue later when you have both calmed down.

- Listen without getting defensive.

- Inform them that you care about their concerns.

- Be empathetic and understanding about their feelings.

- Avoid escalating the situation.

- Confirm with your partner that you have a correct understanding of their feelings and situation.

Get to understand your partner's feelings first before offering any solutions. This is especially important for women. Women usually need to be understood, while men generally desire solutions. The aim is not conflict avoidance but simply handling contentious issues calmly and respectfully.

Assessing your Social Relationships

Being emotionally intelligent can also benefit your social relationships. Practicing emotional intelligence skills is definitely less complicated in social than romantic relationships.

Emotional skills can help you improve your interpersonal relationships, which in turn lead to better friendships. It is, therefore, important to find the right balance of interpersonal (social) skills and emotional skills. Interpersonal skills are used when interacting with strangers and people who you aren't close with. Emotional skills are used when dealing with people whom you are closer or intimate with.

If you are not careful, you can find yourself going to either one of two extremes. You may be too aloof and distant, or you may be too emotional and willing to share personal information with strangers. You need to have the emotional intelligence to find the right balance.

Some people are naturals when it comes to knowing just how much to share with others. The rest have to figure it out by watching how socially successful people behave around others. If you find it difficult to get the balance right, you should look at likable characters, whether it is on TV or real life, and see how they share the right amount of information with the right people.

Another way is to use your life experiences to determine how to maintain a good relationship. An emotionally intelligent person is able to appreciate the rules of social relationships, both theoretically and practically. Having theoretical interpersonal skills means you know the rules and how they operate. For example, there are times you can tell the status of people's relationship by looking at their behavior.

Practical interpersonal skills involve being able to go ahead and start nurture and maintain a healthy relationship. This requires a daily commitment in communicating and relating to others.

You need to have both the theoretical as well as the practical skills to improve your emotional intelligence. They will make a huge difference in how you build and maintain good social relationships.

Chapter 6: Developing Emotional Intelligence for the Workplace

Emotional intelligence can make a big difference in how you relate to colleagues, bosses, and subordinates. It can also make a key difference in being a good leader, and creating a working environment that is emotionally intelligent. This chapter covers all this and more.

Controlling Workplace Feelings

Some people believe that the workplace is no place for emotions. However, unless you can leave a portion of your brain behind at home, you are going to feel something while at work. The important thing is to manage your emotions so that they don't get the best of you. If you lose control of them, you will experience stress that will gradually make you emotionally unaware. This will not help your career at all.

We have discussed just how important it is to get in touch with your feelings. You may still experience anger or frustration at work, but emotionally intelligent people know how to handle their emotions at the workplace, thus being able to effectively change what they feel.

If you get angry at work, you need to stop and think. It could be caused by a rude client, an obnoxious colleague, or a grumpy and unappreciative boss. The moment those feelings start to rise up inside you and interfere with your work, use the following questions to get a grip on the situation:

1. **What is it that upset me?** Size up the event that upset you and check whether you are blowing it out of proportion. Think of how to make the situation better. Think of whether the event will mean anything to you five years down the road.

2. **What about the event is upsetting?** Ask yourself whether the same event would have upset your colleagues. Maybe it is your interpretation of the situation that is the problem. The solution is to examine the event that upset you and change some of the variables. For example, ask yourself whether it would have upset somebody else as much as it did you. Would the impact have been the same had the timing been different?

3. **Why do I still feel angry?** To get over long-term grudges with co-workers, try converting the extreme negative emotion into a more neutral feeling. For example, if you are very upset, change it to mild frustration.

4. **Is being upset helpful in any way**? Excessive negative emotions can damage you both psychologically and physically. The best way to deal with negative feelings is to turn the extreme emotion into a mild feeling. It also helps to reinterpret the situation. For example, maybe your boss shouted you down because he is insecure about you taking his job and not because you are bad at your job.

5. **Is being upset damaging to me?** Think of how your reactions will negatively affect the situation and your standing in the workplace. Punching walls, throwing files around, and overturning tables isn't smart at all. The solution is to visualize someone who is extremely angry with you. Do they look flattering at all, and would you want to associate with such a person?

6. **How do I start to calm down?** The best way is to take a step back and withdraw from the situation. This would be a good time to pull out some positive affirmations and read them out loud in a quiet place. You can also count slowly from one to ten, and use visualization technique to think up peaceful and serene scenes.

7. **Is my communication with colleagues effective when I'm upset?** Extreme negative emotions tend to turn all your focus on the problems facing you, thus hindering your communication with colleagues. The solution is to calm down using any of the methods described in chapter 4. Then think of the situation from the perspective of the other party in the conflict and why they acted the way they did. This may be difficult but you should try it first before confronting them.

Managing Other's Emotions in the Workplace

Most managers try to influence subordinates by ordering them around. The problem with this approach is that it breeds feelings of resentment. You are better off making a request and making the employee feel like part of the team. Managers who are emotionally intelligent have the following attributes:

- They do not issue orders

- They explain the reasons for their request

- They speak to their employees like team members rather than subordinates

- They explain how both parties will benefit from the request

- They make sure that the interaction leaves the employee with a positive feeling

These tips will help you manage the emotions of other people around the workplace.

How to Improve Work Performance in a People-Oriented Job

If you have a people-oriented job where you interact with others, you need to learn how to be a people-person. You need to know how to deal effectively with people if you want to succeed in the workplace.

There are some tips that you can follow in case you are dealing with colleagues who aren't easy to get along with:

- Understand your working style. Consider whether there are specific people who you don't get along with or whether you just don't like working with others. If there are people who bother you, simply reorganize your work tasks around them.

- Know how you feel. If you know that there are some people that you prefer to work with over others, schedule your work so that you spend more time with those you get along with.

- Choose the time of day when you are most comfortable dealing with that person.

- Choose the place where you are most comfortable interacting with that person.

- Plan your interactions with them in advance so that you will be able to control the situation.

- Keep your interactions as short as possible.

- Act professionally at all times. Immaturity and being rude at the workplace is unprofessional.

When dealing with people who you do not get along with at work, try to be polite and professional. Plan the interaction in advance and rehearse the scenario prior to meeting them. This will make the actual encounter much easier.

Emotionally Intelligent Leadership

Every leader is called to rise to the occasion and show good leadership. A leader who possesses the necessary emotional skills will definitely have a greater chance of being successful in the workplace. If you are a leader, it means you already have the technical and intellectual competencies required to do the job. However, without emotional intelligence, you may not stay a leader for long.

So what are some of the social and emotional factors you need to keep in mind as a leader at work? Here are a few things to keep in mind:

1. Get to know and understand your employees.
Always pay attention to the people you are working with. Take the time to understand how they think, their strengths, weaknesses, likes, and dislikes. Talk to them about their feelings about the work they do and make them feel included when making decisions that will affect them. You don't have to agree with their input, but at least hear what they have to say.

2. Embrace social responsibility
A study conducted by the Center for Creative Leadership showed that leaders who are successful tend to be more socially responsible. You should consider ways of becoming more socially responsible, and show your workmates that you care for the local community at large. Bring your team together and find ways to help those within the community who are in need.

3. Practice utmost integrity
Every leader who wants to be respected must earn it. You cannot demand respect yet you do not show any integrity. Be a person who says what they mean, means what they say, and acts according to their word. If you cannot keep your word for some reason, explain to those involved. This will earn you their trust and respect - two attributes that researchers have found to be critical aspects of good leadership.

4. Show empathy
An empathetic leader is one who listens to his team. Listening skills are important if you want to make people feel valued and worth your time.

5. Show assertiveness
This is not the same as being aggressive. Assertiveness means standing for what you believe in and refusing to be moved. A successful leader must be decisive, and if you do not know how to solve a problem, ask others for advice. Finally, an assertive leader must be able to confidently deliver bad news to his team without fear.

6. Be visionary and optimistic

Your team will not follow you if you do not have a clear vision of where you want them to go. A leader should spread optimism especially when things get dark so that people are inspired to keep following the vision.

7. Surround yourself with the best people

Too many leaders are mediocre simply because they choose to surround themselves with allies who are loyal yet incompetent. A good leader knows that when challenges come, you will need people who have the skills to help out. You need to pick people whose skills complement your own so that your team is well rounded and complete.

If you want to become a successful leader at your workplace, you will need to work on your emotional skills. Being emotionally intelligent makes a big difference because leadership is something that you practice everywhere you go – at work, in the home, or even in your social circles. Develop your emotional and social skills and become a better leader.

Conclusion

Most people usually underrate emotional intelligence because we tend to put more emphasis on intellectual competency. We hope that you have been convinced just how important it is to invest in your emotional intelligence. This book has given you a great foundation for learning more about how to increase your emotional intelligence and EQ.

Emotional intelligence is a very wide field and though this book has done a great job of starting you off, it is important to read as many different resources as you can. Put into practice the information you have learned here and invest in your emotional intelligence. It is one decision you will never regret!

Welcome to the BONUS page!

https://thetreplife.leadpages.co/benjamin-smith-limitless-mind/

>>FREE BONUS<<

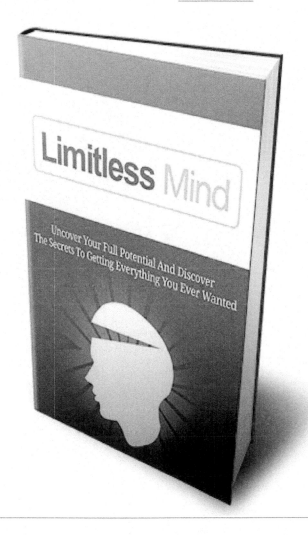

Resources

www.unh.edu
www.psychologytoday.com
www.cleverbridge.my
www.dummies.com

CPSIA information can be obtained
at www.ICGtesting.com
Printed in the USA
LVOW13s1547160217

524503LV00009B/725/P